The Joy of Being Being 50 plus

Written by Allia Zobel
Illustrated by Roz Chast

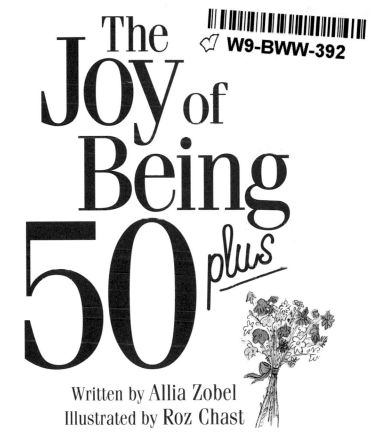

WORKMAN PUBLISHING, NEW YORK

Library of Congress Cataloging-in-Publication Data
Zobel, Allia.
The joy of being fifty plus/by Allia Zobel; illustrated by Roz Chast
p. cm.
ISBN 0-7611-1310-X
1. Middle aged women—Humor.
2. Middle aged women—Cartoons and caricatures.
I. Title.
PN6231.M47Z62   1999
741.5'973—dc21   98-53910
CIP

Workman books are available at special discounts when purchased in bulk for premiums and sales promotions as well as for fund-raising or educational use. Special editions or book excerpts can also be created to specification. For details, contact the Special Sales Director at the address below.

Workman Publishing
708 Broadway
New York, New York 10003-9555
Manufactured in the United States of America
First Printing May 1999

For God; my parents, Alvin and Lucille; my husband, Desmond Finbarr Nolan; my 94-years-young new-old-friend, Eugene Meyer; and all the fifty-year-olds celebrating their forty-ninth again this year.

—Allia Zobel

To Rita Rosenkranz, Peter Workman, Sally Kovalchick, and booksellers everywhere, a huge thanks for your support. With a small book and a name that ends in "z," I need all the help you've always given me.

—A.Z.

It's common knowledge that it's not age but attitude that counts. So, since you're going to turn 50 anyway (some people more than once), it makes more sense to treat the occasion as a milestone. Celebrate in a big way. Blow your own horn (if you have enough wind). Beat your own drum (arthritis permitting). Concentrate (if you can) on the pluses—things like free junkets to retirement villages in the Carolinas and being able to light campfires with your reading glasses.

By the time you're 50, you can do all the things Mom said you couldn't until you were a grown-up. You can leave the table without permission, stay up all night and watch TV, and invite dates in after the movies. And, since people can't threaten to snitch on you to your mother anymore, you can do all the things you've always wanted to do: drink soda and let a burp rip, get a puppy and set a place for her at the table, and play connect the dots with your age spots. That's because 50's the perfect age to quit trying to be perfect, and to stop taking yourself so seriously.

Admitting you're 50 frees up a lot of the time and energy that formerly went into keeping the fact you *are* 50 a secret.

You can stop memorizing a different date of birth, showing your passport with your thumb obscuring your age, trying to white out the numbers on your baptismal certificate and pretending you've lost your license when anyone asks you for identification.

Truth is, there's plenty of joy in being 50—if you're open to it. It's the perfect time for folks to do whatever it is they have in their hearts to do—or not to do. After all, anyone who's lived half a century has earned the right. Think of it: No one can tell you to grow up anymore!

Enjoy!

—Allia Zobel

You can be eccentric.

Your children will start to be nice to you.

You can talk to yourself as much as
you want to—or not at all.

No one will think it's odd if you
start feeding the pigeons.

It's okay to pinch the cheeks of young men at parties.

You can go on a spending spree with
your pension-plan money.

You can reorganize your bathroom cabinet.

People will assume you know everything.

You won't need an excuse to take
naps with your cats.

You can take up knitting again.

You can reminisce out loud.

People will compliment you on how
good you look for your age.

THE SPIKED HEEL HEAVE-HO

No way, pal.

All pain, no gain.

I don't *think* so.

Manolo Blah-WHO?

You can put lots of doilies on your couch.

People will understand if you forget
why you came into the room.

When it comes to your hair, you have oodles of options.

Electrocution
Purple

A Striped Zebra

Barbara Bush
White

You don't have
to hold in your
stomach if you
don't want to.

You can stop taking yourself so seriously.

You can speak
from experience.

You can hold complaining
contests with your friends.

You can brag to friends if a
construction worker whistles at you.

Sneaking prunes will be a thing of the past.
Now you can eat them around the clock.

You'll have a different reunion
to go to every week.

You'll be eligible for the senior
synchronized swimming team.

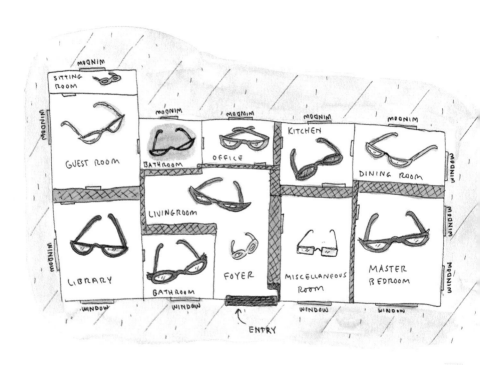

You can splurge on a different pair of reading
glasses for every room in the house.

You can make love like a bunny—
without a care.

Choosing face creams will be a real hoot.

VITAMIN L² CRÈME

AWAY! ANTI-AGER

PURE MAPLE SYRUP LOTION

Ground Antelope Toenail REPLENISHING MASQUE

MOTOR OIL For You

GOAT EMBRYO REVITALIZING WRINKLE RELAXER

BEAUTY PLUS. PEANUT-BUTTER-AND-JELLY MASQUE

B222-C06 BEE POLLEN LOTION

SPIED CRÈME

CHINS BE-GONE

GUACAMOLE FACE CREAM

You can surf 50-plus chat rooms openly.

You can ask grocery boys to help
you with your packages.

You can watch TV programs rated
"for mature audiences only."

It's okay to be
absent-minded.

You can begin a 50-and-over herbal tea group.

You can get your face lifted—
or your whole body.

Casinos and bus-tour
companies will treat you royally.

You're old enough to be a grouch.

You can hire the neighbor's kid
to help you thread needles.

You can buy a Winnebago with the money you would have spent on feminine protection, and donate your early pregnancy test kits to charity for a tax deduction.

Goodbye, "Living" Bras!

Who Wears Short Shorts? Who cares?

Adios, Control-Panel Girdle!

Sayonara, Thong!

Off to Goodwill, Spike Heels!

Adieu, Micro-Miniskirt!

When it comes to clothes, you can dress for ease and comfort. Throw away your living bras and "hold-it-all-in" panty girdle. Never wear a garter belt unless you want to. Ditch the mini-skirts and tight sweaters in favor of long skirts, "big" jewelry, and Birkenstocks. Even better, you'll look divine in hats and sunglasses.

You can purchase birthday candles in bulk.

You can check your cholesterol and blood
pressure all day long and no one
will think you're a hypochondriac.

You can get a tattoo and chalk it up
to a hormonal imbalance.

Your nieces will beg you to teach them
retro dances—like The Lindy, The Twist
or The Pony—at family weddings.

You don't have to wax your
bikini line if you don't want to.

You can (finally) tell Mom
you're too old to wear matching outfits.

You can repeat yourself, you can repeat yourself, and no one will think anything of it.

You can start an exotic scarf collection to
camouflage the hint of chicken neck.

You can take up ballroom dancing.

People will understand if you're
hot one minute and cold the next.

You don't have to pretend you don't
know the words to the golden oldies.

You can earn extra money by
participating in interesting focus groups.

You can buy a loaded Harley and blame your midlife crisis.

No one will mind if you fall
asleep at the dinner table.

All-you-can-eat-except-the-ship cruises
will appeal to you, as will polka-dotted
swimsuits with pleated skirts.

You can pretend you're 49
and people might still believe you.

You don't have to hide your
grandchildren when company visits.

You can cancel your subscription
to *Playgirl,* or perhaps start one.

You can nip at the sherry bottle and say it's for your circulation.

If your figure
goes south, you
can go with it.

You can revel in a second childhood.

You can become an Earth Mother
and spend all your time on pet causes.

If you get a pimple, you'll applaud.

You can trade spandex and the pump-and-preen scene for a loose-fitting tracksuit and an early morning mall-walking group.

You can take early retirement and catalog your collection of beauty-parlor rain hats, film containers, empty Mrs. Butterworth's syrup bottles, and those cute little scoops you get inside coffee containers. What's more, no one will bat an eyelash if you walk away with extra napkins or packets of sugar and ketchup.

You can wear reinforced-toe knee-highs,
and take advantage of support panty hose sales.

You can begin your memoirs.

You can make plans for your centennial.

ABOUT THE AUTHOR

ALLIA ZOBEL is a free-lance writer whose work has appeared in the *New York Times,* the *Washington Post, New Woman* magazine, and dozens of other newspapers and magazines. She is the author of *The Joy of Being Single, 101 Reasons Why a Cat Is Better than a Man, Women Who Love Cats too Much* and six other humor books.

ABOUT THE ILLUSTRATOR

ROZ CHAST has been a cartoonist for *The New Yorker* for the past 19 years. She is the illustrator for *The Joy of Being Single* and is also the author of *Proof of Life on Earth* and five other cartoon collections.